W9-ALM-552

# Christian Heritage
# TEACHING GUIDE
## The Salem Years

# Nancy Rue

## BETHANY HOUSE PUBLISHERS
MINNEAPOLIS, MINNESOTA 55438

J372.89
RUE

*Christian Heritage Series Teaching Guide, The Salem Years*
Copyright © 1998
Nancy N. Rue

Cover illustration by Cheri Bladholm
Cover design by Bradley Lind
Inside design by Sherry Paavola

This author is represented by the literary agency of Alive Communications, 1465
Kelly Johnson Blvd., Suite 320, Colorado Springs, CO 80920.

A Focus on the Family book
Published by Bethany House Publishers
A Ministry of Bethany Fellowship International
11300 Hampshire Avenue South
Minneapolis, Minnesota 55438

Printed in the United States of America by
Bethany Press International, Minneapolis, Minnesota 55438

Library of Congress Cataloging-in-Publication Data
Rue, Nancy N.
    The Christian heritage series teaching guide/Nancy Rue.
        p. cm.
Contents: The Salem years
    ISBN 1-56179-640-9
    1. Reading (Elementary) 2. Language arts (Elementary) 3. Education,
Elementary—Activity programs. 4. Puritans—Study and teaching (Elementary) 5.
American history—Study and teaching (Elementary) I. title.
LB1573.R727        1998
372.4—dc21                                                    98-27229
                                                    CIP

98 99 00 01 02/10 9 8 7 6 5 4 3 2 1

# Contents

# Teacher to Teacher

Whether you have 35 desks in your classroom or two chairs pulled up to the dining room table, you have an extremely valuable job to do. I know—I've been in your shoes. I've done more teaching than just about anything else, including eating frozen yogurt, reading suspense novels, and driving my sports car with *The Lion King* soundtrack blasting (which are my other passions). I've spent 16 years teaching in public schools, five years leading creative dramatics workshops, 19 years (to date) mentoring my budding-author daughter, and all the while I have continuously tutored one-on-one. My entire adult life has been spent sharing what I know with kids and learning with them as we explore, discover, and create.

I've learned two important things from those 21 years in education:

1. Teaching is hard work.
2. Teachers need all the help we can get, no matter how good at it we already are.

Unfortunately, most of us educators are usually so swamped that we don't have time to even think about sharing the materials we *have* had a chance to discover. That's why I've developed this teaching guide to accompany The Christian Heritage Series. It's my way of propping open my classroom door and pulling out my idea files for you to dig through.

Inside you'll find materials designed for kids from third to eighth grade. I hope you'll be able to use them, whether you're teaching public school kids, Christian school students, or your own offspring. The guide is organized the following way:

**History Folder:** Gives a quick rundown on the historical background for The Salem Years and presents activities for tying *The Rescue, The Stowaway, The Guardian, The Accused, The Samaritan,* and *The Secret* into your study of American history.

**Literature Folder:** Explains a basic element of literature illustrated in each book, with suggested activities for reinforcing the literary concepts. (These are continued in the subsequent guides for The Williamsburg Years and The Charleston Years.)

**Writing Folder:** Presents tons of ideas for getting pens into your students' hands. These activities key into the books' themes and the ways they relate to children's lives today. They're presented in skill-building order.

**Christianity Folder:** Provides a review of what was happening in the church at the time of the stories as well as what can be learned about God in each book. The teaching guide can be used by public school educators as a history of religion in America and as support for studying basic values. Christian schoolteachers and homeschool parents can use them directly as illustrations of people living—or not living—their Christian principles.

**Ways-to-Make-It-Matter Folder:** Gives a file of activities that students in each of the three levels (third/fourth grades, fifth/sixth grades, and seventh/eighth grades) can do at the end of the six-book series to pull together what they've learned about literature, history, themselves, and God. The ideas can be used "as is" or lead to just-perfect projects you and your kids design together.

**Feel-Free-to-Photocopy Folder:** Features reproducible sheets for activities in three levels. These are referred to in the various sections.

**A Word from the Author:** Gives ways our young readers can communicate with me. I'd love to get their feedback!

It's my prayer that this guide will assist you in the work you're doing with young people. I consider teaching to be one of the most important, vital jobs a person can have. I also hope it will inspire you—*and* your students—to reach new heights of creativity. After all, that's what reading books is all about. Enjoy!

Nancy Rue
Author of The Christian Heritage Series

# A Few Facts About The Salem Years

- All of the history surrounding the events in the stories is accurate.
- The tension between Salem Village and Salem Town did exist as depicted in the books.
- The following people lived in Salem in 1690-91, and their characters in these stories are based on what I have read about their actual personalities (the specific events and conversations, of course, are fictional): John and Elizabeth Proctor; Reverend Samuel Parris, his wife, their daughter, Betty, and their niece Abigail Williams; Tituba and John Indian; Thomas, John, Edward, and Nathaniel Putnam and their half brother Joseph Putnam; Israel Porter; Francis and Rebecca Nurse; Ezekiel Cheever; John Willard; Reverend Nicholas Noyes; Reverend Higginson; Phillip and Mary English; Dr. Griggs; and Nathaniel Hathorne.
- The Salem Years end before the infamous Salem witch trials took place, but the events you will read about in these books set the stage for that dark time in our history.
- The books can be read as individual stories but are probably most appreciated when enjoyed in order as one big story.
- All the books in The Christian Heritage Series are written for enjoyment and understanding, not for memorizing characters'

names or other tedious forms of literary torture! You won't find any read-the-chapter-and-answer-the-questions kinds of assignments here. The activities are designed to help your students enjoy learning—after all, students of all ages learn best when they're having fun and exercising their imaginations.

*Note:* In the **Feel-Free-to-Photocopy Folder**, there is a history sheet for each book for each grade level to be used in addition to or instead of the activity given for each book in the History Folder. This gives you options, depending on how much time you want to spend on each book and area.

# The 𝕽escue

It's spring 1690 when The Salem Years begin. It's been 70 years since the Pilgrims landed at Plymouth Rock in 1620 and began their settlement in the New World. Men like Josiah's fictitious grandfather thought of the new Massachusetts as God's own colony. They came to create an ideal state, a place where they were free to worship as they pleased and govern themselves without interference. It seemed that their dream would come true. In spite of the hardships of winter, deaths from disease and starvation, and the challenge of getting along with the Indians, many Puritans felt that they lived in a place where everyone believed in the same thing—the almighty power of God. They followed strict rules in their society, which they had to do because times were so rough; the laws gave them security and made the colony a safe place to live. But changes began to crowd in.

In 1664, England's new king, Charles II, had sent a commission to the colony with orders to assert royal power over Massachusetts. The Puritans became nervous and wanted to protect what little freedom and security they had. So just as they were persecuted by the Church of England in the past, *they* began to persecute anyone who was not of *their* faith, particularly the Quakers. They thought that any religion different from their own would try to squash them as the Church of England had done—even the peaceful Quakers!

At the same time, farming land was becoming scarce. The Puritans had mostly been farmers, living off the land since their arrival—but some were forced to begin working in the trade and shipping industries to support themselves. That change gave rise to much dissension within the church, and it led to the conflict between Salem Town and Salem Village, which you will read about in The Salem Years books. As Massachusetts became a safer, more civilized place, some members of the church no longer saw the need for such strict regulations; others thought it was a sin to change anything. Thus, the beginning of The Salem Years depicts a very unsettled society. As Josiah's father, Joseph Hutchinson, puts it in *The Rescue*, "They've forgotten why our fathers and grandfathers came here" (p. 113).

**DOMESTIC DETAILS IN *THE RESCUE* INCLUDE:** rules against swimming, the discipline of children, children's chores, kids' games, planting crops, perils of transportation, illness and medicine, and public punishment.

## HISTORY ACTIVITIES FOR *THE RESCUE*

### Third/Fourth:
Playing the way Puritan children did will help you to "experience" history. Spend one day or a recess using only the kinds of toys Josiah and his friends used—things such as whistles, soap bubbles, cords for Cat's Cradle, and leaf boats. Those are just a few examples; see what other toys you can find in the book. Remember, no TV or computer games allowed. Don't use anything that couldn't have been found "back then." Then report to the class or teacher what it was like being a 17th-century kid for a day!

### Fifth/Sixth:
Find out more about one of the southern New England Indian tribes—the Wampanoags, the Narragansets, or the Nipmucks. Write a paragraph about a friendship you might have had with a Native American child from that tribe.

### Seventh/Eighth:
Josiah's grandfather's decision to leave England and come to the New World affected Josiah's whole life. See if you can find out how your family came to North America. Create a timeline or draw diagrams on a map. Be creative—make it fun! On the back, write about how their decision to come here has affected *you*. In other words, what might your life be like if your ancestors *hadn't* left their native country? Or, if you are Native American and your distant relatives were originally from the New World, what do you imagine life would be like for you if they had emigrated to another country?

# The Stowaway

Josiah spends the summer in Salem Town so he can learn more about "city" life in 17th-century Massachusetts, particularly concerning the shipping industry. Due to a decision by the General Court, all goods shipped in or out of the colony had to pass through either Boston or Salem, so Salem Town was quite a busy harbor. The people living there were basically ruled by the ocean tides. Most were merchants who worked at sending cod and mackerel, furs and horses, and grains and meat to the other colonies and to the West Indies and the Canary Islands.

The farmers living near Josiah's family had formed their own village, but they were still controlled by the City Selectmen of Salem Town. Smart men like Joseph Hutchinson took advantage of the new opportunities and shipped their goods in trade—much to the disapproval of the other village men. Josiah's father, seeing that times were changing, was adamant that Josiah be educated so he could make good decisions rather than remain ignorant like many of the village people.

But although there was a law decreed by the Massachusetts General Court in 1647 that every settlement of 50 families or more had to have public schools for its children, there was no school in Salem Village. Most of the Puritans there thought that as long as their children were taught the proper religious doctrine, they would grow up to be good citizens—with or without a formal education. There were summer dame schools for small children, but men like Joseph Hutchinson who were concerned about schooling had to either send their older sons away to grammar school or hire tutors, something most could not afford.

In *The Stowaway*, Josiah goes to stay with ship owner Phillip English, who was an actual citizen of Salem Town, while getting his education. English owned a fleet of 21 ships, had constructed 14 buildings, lived with his wife, Mary, in a mansion on Essex

Street, and was known for carrying an elegant white beech cane with an ivory handle and gold trim. During his stay with English in Salem Town, Josiah also meets Joseph Putnam, who was in reality the kindhearted half brother of the evil Putnams.

DOMESTIC DETAILS IN *THE STOWAWAY* INCLUDE: crop plagues, eating habits, courtship, highway robbery, shipping, discipline of kids, the traditional house-raising, and prating for pigeons.

## HISTORY ACTIVITIES FOR *THE STOWAWAY*

Third/Fourth:
   When Josiah goes back to Salem Village, he eventually tells William and Ezekiel everything he's learned about ships, but since he still doesn't like to talk much, he draws a picture of the ketch *The Adventure* and labels it. Draw a diagram of something that interests you as Josiah did and show it to one of your friends.

Fifth/Sixth:
   Write a budding sailor's guidebook, including all the things Josiah learned about ships during his summer stay in Salem Town.

Seventh/Eighth:
   Pretend you're giving an 11-year-old kid from the 17th century the choice to study farming or explore the sea. He needs a fair presentation of the pros and cons of each profession, based on facts. Tell him these facts in some creative way—maybe in poster form, in an informative speech, or by tape-recording a dramatic dialogue.

# The Guardian

In the larger world of New England, war raged with the Indians, particularly in Maine. The fighting had a profound effect on individuals as far away as Massachusetts. Widows whose husbands had been killed in battle had to go all the way to Boston and pay high fines to claim their spouse's property. That was because 26 years before, Oliver Cromwell, champion of the Puritans, had died in England, and Charles II had come to the throne.

The new king had sent a commission to the colony to assert royal power over the people of Massachusetts. The king's people stirred up the Indians and took away the colonists' charter for governing themselves. Although the royal tyrant Governor Andros was overthrown in 1690, the new governor, Simon Bradstreet, was worse because he couldn't seem to do anything at all. Increase Mather, a Puritan leader, had been in England for three years trying to get King James, who succeeded Charles II, to approve a charter. But in the midst of that, King James was replaced by William and Mary—who were already angry with the colonists for overthrowing Andros.

During the time *The Guardian* portrays, there was no real charter, no real governor, and no real government in Massachusetts. The insecurity and fear were reflected in Salem Village, where unfortunately, even though there were no hostile Indians, militiamen were being trained in case of attack. This was a definite change. When the Puritans had first arrived in 1620, Captain John Alden of Plymouth had a truce with the Indians and the colony lived in peace with them. The early settlers called the southern New England Indians the "Praying Indians."

Then the colonists became greedy. Traders and property owners broke the truce and took the Indians' land. Some Puritans thought the Indians were the devil's people and saw nothing wrong with stealing their land. Meanwhile, the old-guard Puritans in Boston who were busy running things for Governor Bradstreet were doing nothing to help the colonists in Maine, who were under Indian attack. A parallel war—a cold, silent one—raged within Salem Village. Men dragged their neighbors to court over petty land disputes, waged an unnecessarily cruel battle against the wolves that "threatened" their livestock and property, and tried to control the church because they couldn't control anything else. The settlers were so busy doing sneaky things to frighten others into moving away or to scare them into doing things the colonists' way that they had lost sight of the real reason their fathers had come to the New World.

**DOMESTIC DETAILS IN *THE GUARDIAN* INCLUDE:** dealing with wolves (particularly the wolf rout), Puritan teenagers, apple picking, hay rides, popping corn, nut gathering, and the celebration of Thanksgiving.

## HISTORY ACTIVITIES FOR *THE GUARDIAN*

### Third/Fourth:

Using your own drawings, put together a short picture book on how the early settlers dealt with the animals that threatened their lives or farms. You can create your book using only the information about wolves in *The Guardian*, or you can read about other animals that affected the early settlers, such as bears, snakes, raccoons, locusts, and mountain lions. Even skunks might be fun!

### Fifth/Sixth:

Draw a totem pole on paper (or create one with clay) that shows the changes in the settlers' relationships with the Indians from the beginning of the Massachusetts colony to Josiah's time. You can use just the facts you've gathered from the first three books, or you can do some more research and add information by looking up the Wampanoag, Narraganset, and Nipmunk Indians. Be creative and use symbols or pictures to describe the changes that took place in early colonial times.

Seventh/Eighth:

Women, children, and retarded people were treated much differently than they are now, as you can see in *The Rescue* and *The Guardian*. Create a "photo essay" that shows the improvements in the way these groups of people are treated now. Compare and contrast using pictures from magazines and/or your own drawings or symbols.

 # The Accused

In the winter of 1691, tension grew in Salem Village. As in many New England settlements, there were arguments over who owned what property and who had damaged certain land. Since land was the people's means of survival, neighbors would often drag one another to court without batting an eye. Courtrooms were austere places, and jails were worse. Cases might have been handled more swiftly than they are now—but justice wasn't always served. Few people were allowed lawyers, and decisions were sometimes based on a person's influence in town. Those convicted, whether they were actually guilty or not, suffered in miserable jail conditions, as Abigail Williams describes in *The Accused*.

At the same time, slaves, particularly from the West Indies, had also made an appearance, having been brought on ships by Boston and Salem traders. Society was definitely changing, and every person had to decide whether to change with it, and how much.

DOMESTIC DETAILS IN *THE ACCUSED* INCLUDE: carding wool, the firewood situation, sledding, fires, fences, staying warm, and sleigh rides.

## HISTORY ACTIVITIES FOR *THE ACCUSED*

### Third/Fourth:

Help a grown-up fix a winter supper like the Hutchinsons would have eaten. Use the book to help plan the menu, and if you have a fireplace, eat beside it. You might try eating the entire meal with a spoon, since the colonists didn't have forks yet!

### Fifth/Sixth:

Find out more about West Indian slaves in the 17th century. Then write a description of what you think Tituba's and John Indian's life might have been like before they came to Massachusetts. Also explain how they were taken to the New World.

### Seventh/Eighth:

Read up on the New England Indians (Wampanoags, Narragansets, Nipmucks). Pick a tribe, then create a gift an Indian from the tribe you chose might have given Josiah.

# The Samaritan

In spite of God's abundant land in New England, there were many poor and even starving people in Massachusetts in 1691 who were driven to begging at back doors to survive. Many of those who were well-off believed their wealth was God's blessing on them—and that poverty for others was His curse. Instead of helping the poor find their way, these "stiff-necked people," as Josiah's father calls them, spent their time jealously guarding their property and dragging to court anyone who set foot on it without an invitation. Even the minister tried to claim the land the church was on as his own! Such greed was tearing more and more people away from their beliefs, and so the basis for their society—Christianity—continued to crumble.

**DOMESTIC DETAILS IN *THE SAMARITAN* INCLUDE:** dealing with bears, superstitions, removing stumps for plowing, quilt making, beating the bounds, carrying weapons, tightening a bed, a Puritan funeral, dress-up clothes, and the town ordinary.

## HISTORY ACTIVITIES FOR *THE SAMARITAN*

Third/Fourth:
"Beat the bounds" of your property with your mom or dad (although you can leave out the beating part!). Even if you live in an apartment or a condo with a yard the size of a postage stamp, together take stock of all you have and give thanks for it. Celebrate it! You can even draw a wonderful picture of your family's "property" (home) to remind you of how blessed you really are.

Fifth/Sixth:
Find out more about bear problems in the early settlements.

18

(Ask a librarian for help if you need to.) Use the information you find to create your own short story about a young boy or girl's confrontation with a 17th- or 18th-century bear.

Seventh/Eighth:
Find out more about the treatment of the poor and of abandoned children in the 17th century. Make a poster—17th-century style—enlightening the Puritans about what's happening.

# The Secret

Tensions were coming to a head in Salem Village in the summer of 1691. The majority of its citizens were fighting for personal power instead of depending on God's strength and sovereignty to guide them, and their fight centered around the church. Secrets about the Reverend Samuel Parris were uncovered that made him more paranoid than ever. This made some of the Putnams even more anxious to protect Parris, since without their puppet, their power over the church was nonexistent. Such carryings-on created more than good reason for God-loving Christians to move elsewhere to pursue their dream of a godly society. Some went to Rhode Island and Connecticut, while others left New England completely. New York and even Delaware and Virginia began to grow as more dissatisfied settlers left Massachusetts.

**DOMESTIC DETAILS IN *THE SECRET* INCLUDE:** using flint to start a fire, medical procedures, and dealing with snakes.

## HISTORY ACTIVITIES FOR *THE SECRET*

### Third/Fourth:

Get yourself a sheet of paper and write a message describing the most important thing you've learned about life in 17th-century Massachusetts from reading The Salem Years, or just from *The Secret*. For fun, write with charred wood or berry juice (try grape juice with a fine paintbrush).

### Fifth/Sixth:

Put together a medical guidebook for the Puritan in 17th-century Massachusetts, using the cures and treatments you've learned in The Salem Years. Or, if you'd prefer, write up a first-aid sheet using only information from *The Secret*.

### Seventh/Eighth:

Put together a guide for surviving The Salem Years—1690–91—in Massachusetts. Make sure you cover important subjects such as Indians, the importance of land and education, the sad reality of hunger and poverty, how Christians should respond to corruption and fighting in the church, how to make a living in trade and/or farming, and any other significant areas the books from The Salem Years present.

# The Rescue

Since to me a novel isn't worth reading unless it tells an absorbing story, let's consider *plot* first. Plot is *what happens* in a story. It depicts how things happen, and it makes what happens interesting. I've listed my suggestions below for approaching plot in *The Rescue*:

Third/Fourth:

Concentrate on what happens and in what order. You can do this by summarizing the chapters together. Play a group trivia game with the important events that occur in *The Rescue*. Or put the things that happen in a chapter on cards, mix them up, and put them back in order. Those are good ways to home in on plot. You could even use these plot exercises for all six books if you're so inclined. In the Feel-Free-to-

Photocopy Folder, you'll find a Plot sheet to use if you want to continue working on plot in *The Rescue* (p. 70).

## Fifth/Sixth:

Kids this age are ready to look at how a plot is put together. Usually it goes something like this (see diagram):

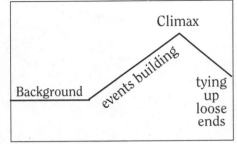

You might want to keep a big "plot line" on the board or on a poster as you read and fill it in together. In the Feel-Free-to-Photocopy section, you'll find one for students to complete (p. 72).

## Seventh/Eighth:

I suggest discussing *conflict* with your seventh and eighth grader(s) since they seem to generate it in their own lives! You might talk about how no story is interesting if things just roll along smoothly and everyone gets along famously. Point out how boring their favorite movie or TV show would be without an argument, car chase, or court battle. If you really want to get literary, you can discuss the fact that there are categories of conflict in literature:

• Person versus nature (for example, a snowstorm that traps everyone inside for a week)
• Person versus person (for example, a quarrel between siblings)
• Person versus society (for example, an innocent person sentenced to a life term in prison)
• Person versus himself (for example, a person who, knowingly or not, does things to harm himself, such as procrastinating so badly that he receives a failing grade in a class)

*The Rescue* is loaded with conflict. The Plot sheet in the Feel-Free-to-Photocopy section will help your student(s) identify and sort out the different conflicts that surface in this book (p. 73).

# The Stowaway

Since *The Stowaway* is set in a different place than the other books in The Salem Years, it seems like the perfect time to talk about *setting*, which is the *where and when* of a story. We talk at length about the *when* in the history section, so let's focus on the *where* now.

### Third/Fourth:

There's a lot to discuss! How is Salem Village different from Salem Town? In which area would you rather live? Can you find pictures of 17th-century ships? Can you locate books in the library that have pictures of Salem Town in the 1690s? Pick out some sections in which the author describes a place and draw the picture that comes to your mind. Try pages 75-82 or pages 97-98 in *The Stowaway*. You could also fill out the Setting sheet in the Feel-Free-to-Photocopy Folder as you read (p. 74).

### Fifth/Sixth:

Sometimes the best part of reading a book is filling in the setting details in your mind. In some places, the author gives you just a few specifics, and you have to use your imagination for the rest. For example, in *The Stowaway*, we know only that Josiah's bedroom at the Englishes' house has a high bed with embroidered curtains and a mountain of cushions (p. 47). Can you mentally fill in the rest? Look up pictures of 17th-century houses and furniture to help you. Then draw a picture or write a description of what you see in your mind.

If you enjoy doing that, find some other places in the book where certain details of the setting are missing. Use the Setting sheet in the Feel-Free-to-Photocopy section to help you (p. 75).

**Seventh/Eighth:**

Think about *how* setting is created. How does an author make a reader feel as if he or she is *there*? Pick a setting description, such as the one of Josiah's first sight of the harbor on pages 75-76, and read it out loud. Ask yourself, *Is there something to appeal to each of my five senses here?* You might explore how the author sometimes doesn't describe a place all at once but instead scatters little details here and there. Gather all the specifics about the Hutchinsons' kitchen in chapters 3 and 4 into one list, paragraph, or drawing. Using the Setting sheet in the Feel-Free-to-Photocopy Folder (p. 76) might also be fun.

# The Guardian

Now that you've looked at plot and setting in The Salem Years, it's a good time to talk about *characters*. Who are they? How do we know what they look and act like? How do they change? What do they teach us? As you work with kids on *character* at any level, I'd suggest treating the "people on the page" as real folks you know. That habit will then transfer to future books your students read, and they'll glean much more from their reading.

**Third/Fourth:**

At this level, it's fun just to get to know the characters as people. Put together a booklet with a construction-paper cover and lots of blank pages stapled inside. Each time you meet a new character, list the author's details and then draw a picture to match. Don't forget the wolf and Elizabeth, the doll. Topics of discussion might include: Which of the characters would you want for a friend and why? Which would you definitely not want for a friend and why? What makes Joseph Putnam such a wonderful teacher? Would you want Deborah and Joseph Hutchinson for parents? What about Nathaniel Putnam for a father? Why or why not? How is Josiah different from the way he was in *The Rescue*?

### Fifth/Sixth:

An author uses a number of methods to create characters. With Josiah, for example, consider facts about him the author tells you, what Josiah says, what he does, statements other characters make about Josiah, and the way other characters respond to him.

Give an example of each method (for one character) using just the first chapter in *The Guardian*. Then, to delve further into the subject of character, you can use the Character Map in the Feel-Free-to Photocopy section (p. 77).

### Seventh/Eighth:

This is a good time to explore the difference between a *dynamic* character (one who changes as the result of what he or she experiences in the book) and a *static* character (one who remains the same). You can illustrate using real people. For example, you could write, "My friend Dennis used to be a jerk in fifth grade but now we're buddies"; or "I used to get along with my sister, but ever since she started high school she's gotten moody"; or even "Everybody else seems to be getting more mature, but I don't feel like I'm going anywhere!" Then, perhaps using the Feel-Free-to-Photocopy Character sheet, select two characters you think have changed between the beginning of book one and the end of book three, and two who have remained stubbornly the same. Trace the changes using pictures, drawings, phrases from the books or your own words—or some other creative combination! (See p. 78.)

# The Accused

We see a story happen through one or more characters' eyes. This is a story's *point of view*—a very important element in fiction. But point of view is not something the young student of literature will automatically recognize. So now is a good time to bring point of view to the light of day!

Third/Fourth:

Talk about which character is present throughout *The Accused*. Whose thoughts do you know? Through whose eyes are you seeing the story? The answer, of course, is Josiah's. Use the Feel-Free-to-Photocopy Point of View sheet for this literary concept (p. 79).

Fifth/Sixth:

One of the best ways to approach point of view is to think about how the story would be different if it were viewed through someone else's eyes. What we would know if Hope were telling us the story? How would we feel about the Hutchinsons if we read *The Accused* from Jonathon Putnam's point of view? What would we understand if it were Ezekiel's story? Again, if you want to go further in depth, the activities in the Feel-Free-to-Photocopy section might help (p. 80).

Seventh/Eighth:

These are the "official" terms for various types of point of view:

• First person: The first person is narrating the story—younger kids call these "I Books."

• Third person limited: The story is told from the point of view of one character, like in The Christian Heritage Series.

• Third person omniscient: We know the thoughts and experiences of all or most of the characters.

Discuss why I, the author, chose third person limited for The Christian Heritage books and how the series would have been different if I had chosen the first-person or third-person-omniscient point of view. The question students often ask at this point is, Who cares? To answer that, try the sheet in the Feel-Free-to-Photocopy section (p. 81).

# The Samaritan

*Style* is a pretty sophisticated part of literature, but I believe even the third and fourth grade reader can appreciate it on a basic level. Under-standing style definitely helps kids to develop their reading tastes. I encourage *you* to encourage *them* to keep exploring literature until they find a style they enjoy reading—even if it isn't The Christian Heritage Series!

Third/Fourth:

Start by bringing out various children's picture books—perhaps Dr. Seuss, Winnie-the-Pooh, Grimm's Fairy Tales, and Serendipity. Spread them out and talk about the differences in the way they look and the way they're written. That's style—and it comes from the writer's personality. You might even talk about what you think Nancy Rue is like after reading five of her books—and write to me to find out if you're right! The checklist in the Feel-Free-to-Photocopy Folder might be fun to use as well (p. 82).

## Fifth/Sixth:

Discuss different houses you have lived in and how they were decorated. Using magazines might help. Try to name the decorative styles—stark and uncluttered, fancy and frilly, sleek and modern, rustic like summer camp, or comfortable and homey. Then see if the author's writing style matches any of those. Is Nancy Rue's style plain like a living room with white walls? Fancy and frilly with tons of descriptive words hanging everywhere? Once you've determined what the author's writing style might be, compare it with the styles of other books you've read together recently. Try to focus on what style each of you prefers, since appreciation and awareness are what it's all about—not counting how many compound sentences and adverbs the author uses! Use the Feel-Free-to-Photocopy Style sheet for fun (p. 83).

## Seventh/Eighth:

Music is a good way to illustrate style. Listen to and/or talk about some of the music you listen to and describe the various styles. Starting with rap, reggae, or hip-hop is fine. But go beyond those as well. For example, The Newsboys are a Christian rock band and so is DC Talk, but they're very different. Describing *how* they're different will help you understand style. Then, after you've identified various elements of style and how they differ from one another, try to determine Nancy Rue's writing style. Go to the Feel-Free-to-Photocopy Folder for guidance (p. 85).

# The Secret

I believe *theme* is simply the answer to the question, "Why did the author write this book?" What was she trying to comment on, bring to your attention, criticize, laugh at, or teach? For kids, nothing can ruin a good book faster than digging for obscure, hidden meanings and far-fetched symbolism. I would love to see you simply encourage your students to decide what the message of the book is and whether that relates to them in any way.

**Third/Fourth:**

Talk about the title. Why was the book called *The Secret*? What did Josiah learn about secrets? Use the Feel-Free-to-Photocopy Theme sheet to get more discussion going (p. 87).

**Fifth/Sixth:**

A good way to approach theme at this level is to ask, How did Josiah change from the beginning to the end of the book? What did he learn? That's the theme. See if you can all agree on one statement—well, maybe two. The Feel-Free-to-Photocopy sheet will help (p. 89). Then make a modern-day collage using magazine pictures, illustrating the lessons to be learned from either just *The Secret* or all six books in The Salem Years.

**Seventh/Eighth:**

If a book doesn't speak to you, it will be pointless—especially to students at the seventh and eighth grade level. So when dealing with theme, try to relate *The Secret* to your life. You might discuss times you've found yourself keeping a dangerous secret. Times when, like Hope and Silas, you found yourself sneaking around to do something you thought was right but you wouldn't be allowed to do if you asked permission.

If you're in a position to do so, you can talk about how to discern God's will, which is another theme in *The Secret*. Encourage one another to sort out a decision by gathering information about what the Bible says or what your parents believe about finding God's will. The less distance there is between your experience of deciding what God desires for you and Josiah and Hope's situation, the better. I purposely didn't include a sheet for seventh and eighth graders on theme because I think it's important to keep it real-to-life and fun!

The following are topics that will motivate kids to express themselves in writing. Use them "as is" or as springboards for your own creativity. No matter how you utilize the ideas, here are a few suggestions to ensure maximum delight and under-standing:

1. Concentrate on one skill at a time, building so that eventually your students will have strong, balanced, basic writing skills. The skill I suggest concentrating on for each book will be given under the titles.

2. Encourage kids to brainstorm a topic first, listing ideas on paper as fast as they can in words and phrases. Have them look the list over and come up with a central idea, crossing out anything that doesn't fit, as well as adding more support. Then cluster the remaining concepts into a few supporting ideas. This exercise will go a long way toward creating focused, detailed, well-organized writing.

3. Let the first draft be rough—with no concern for spelling, punctuation, and so on. Now is the time to deal with content,

organization, and sparkle. If kids don't have to worry about the mechanics at this point, their writing will be more free.

4. Partner students up, if possible, to review rough drafts and consult on clarity, support, and readability. Make revisions.

5. Only after the previous steps are completed is it time to *polish*. Look up those odd spellings. Home in on punctuation, tighten the sentence structure, double-check capitalization. Now that your kids feel proud of their writing, the mechanics will matter to them rather than get in the way of the process.

6. Make your students' writing significant. Read pieces aloud; print them in booklets; post them on the bulletin board. If it's a dialogue, perform it. If it's a letter, send it. If it's a poem, have a reading. Use your imagination to make it as much fun as possible.

# The Rescue

Writing Clearly: Putting the Details in Order

Third/Fourth Topics:
- A fight with your brother or sister
- A day with your best friend
- A time you were telling the truth and your friends didn't believe you
- A situation in which you were accused of something you didn't do
- A circumstance in which you tried to help but goofed things up
- The bravest thing you ever did

Fifth/Sixth Topics:
- The moment you realized someone was your friend
- A time you saw something you thought might be wrong,

but you weren't sure whether to say anything
- A situation where you felt *really* dumb
- A moment when you felt misunderstood by your parents
- The first time you felt your parents really trusted you

**Seventh/Eighth Topics:**
- A moment when you realized you'd rather be with your friends than with your brother or sister
- A confusing situation that forced you to think things through
- A time when you had to deal with a "handicap," like Josiah did with his stuttering or Hope with her hearing loss or William with his shyness
- A person you wanted to be friends with—or actually developed a friendship with—who was considered "taboo" by everyone else
- A moment when you felt your relationship with one of your parents changed—for better or worse

# The Stowaway

Writing Clearly: Giving Lots of Support

**Third/Fourth Topics:**
- What's it like going to your school? Do you like it? Why or why not? (Be sure to give at least three reasons for your answer.)
- What's it like going to your church? Do you look forward to attending? How do they treat the kids? (Give lots of information and explanation.)
- Have you ever been away from home—away from your family? Did you like it? Why or why not? What were three things that you learned from the experience?

- Do you know a bully? Describe him or her (without naming names)—and give at least three examples of the ways he or she bullies other kids.
- Write a letter to a friend who lives someplace else, telling him or her three things you've learned this school year.

## Fifth/Sixth Topics:

- How do you like to learn—by reading, listening, or doing projects? Write about your learning style, using your best learning experience ever to support it.
- Write about how your church handles kids. Do they have enough programs for people your age? What's Sunday school like? (Don't forget those reasons and examples.)
- Why do bullies act the way they do? Do you know any (avoid naming them specifically)? Describe the way they treat people.
- Have you ever felt you messed up so badly that you couldn't tell anybody—even God? Write a letter to your diary, sorting it out as you write.

## Seventh/Eighth Topics:

- Have you ever been in a position in which your parents wouldn't believe your innocence? Why didn't they trust you? Explain.
- Are girls still treated differently from boys these days? Write a persuasive editorial about that, giving concrete reasons for the position you hold.
- How do you feel about bullies? Why do those people act as they do? What's the best way to handle bullies?
- Is Reverend Parris right—are kids basically little savages who have to be civilized by their parents? Why or why not? How would Reverend Parris describe you, and why?

# The Guardian

Writing Clearly: Using Specific Details

## Third/Fourth Topics:

- Tell about a time when you rescued an animal. Give a lot of details so the reader will feel like he or she's there.
- Describe a time when you felt left out by your friends. Give a lot of details.
- Write about a situation when you had to "put up with" an annoying relative or friend of the family.
- Discuss a time when you teased someone or told him or her a "whopper" and were later sorry.
- Have you hurt someone who doesn't know what you've said or done? Write that person a letter of explanation and apology.

## Fifth/Sixth Topics:

- Think about a time when you saw or heard about someone being cruel to animals. Using lots of details, write a protest poem. (It doesn't have to rhyme.)
- Did you ever "get stuck" having to spend time with somebody—your little brother, your mom's best friend's kid—and have your other friends blow you off? Write a letter to your friends about it and tell them what you learned from the experience.
- Write about a time you did the right thing even though it wasn't fun to do.
- Josiah decided he was like the wolves. With what animal do you identify? Write a poem about yourself as an otter or swan or frog or another animal. If you have time, draw or paint a picture to go along with your poem.

## Seventh/Eighth Topics:

- How do you feel about killing animals for food and clothing? Write lyrics about it to match the tune of one of your favorite songs.
- Is there something that kids are doing in your school or community that makes you mad? Maybe vandalizing buildings with graffiti? Stealing spray paint from hardware stores? Selling drugs to younger kids? Forming exclusive cliques? If you and a group of your friends could form a "Merry Band" and change the bad things other kids are doing in your town, what would you plan? Write up your scheme, complete with all the details, and make sure you follow the Merry Band's rules (see *The Guardian*, pp. 129, 132).
- Josiah realizes he and the wolves share many of the same characteristics. With which animal do you have the most in common? Do a little research on the critter you choose. Draw or find a picture and write a detail-rich poem or essay to go with it.

# The Accused

Writing Clearly: Using Comparison

## Third/Fourth Topics:

- Compare the chores you have to do with those required of your brother or sister. Then write a funny poem about the chores you and your siblings must do.
- Compare winter where you live to winter in Salem Village. Compose a few pretty lines you can mount on a paper snowflake.
- Have you ever had a friend let you down, the way Ezekiel did Josiah? Write two paragraphs, one about your friendship before the betrayal happened and one describing your relationship after it happened. Then draw a picture to go with each scenario.

## Fifth/Sixth Topics:

• Are you and one of your brothers or sisters (or cousins or close friends) complete opposites, the way Hope and Josiah are? Write a fun poem about your differences, using this pattern:

> I am oatmeal
> She's Fruit Loops
> I'm a plain butter cookie
> She's a sundae—two scoops
> I'm generic white kneesocks
> She's purple tights
> I'm a hand-painted road sign
> She's neon lights

• Josiah's father says, "Honesty isn't just keeping your tongue from lying . . . It also means telling the complete truth" (*The Accused*, p. 164). What's the difference? Use examples from your own experiences if you can.

• Sometimes it seems easy to forgive somebody for letting you down, as when Josiah forgave Hope. But often it's very hard to let go of your hurt, as Josiah found when he held a grudge against Ezekiel. Pretend you're in Josiah's situation. Write down how you would explain your feelings to both Hope and Ezekiel.

## Seventh/Eighth Topics:

• Pretend you're taking a group of kids to court who have done you and your friends wrong. Write a deposition comparing their activities to your group's.

• Joseph Putnam said, "I am not ashamed of the truth. I would simply prefer that it not be told just yet" (*The Accused*, p. 90). What's the difference? Write a comparison, using examples from your own experiences, if possible.

• On page 197, Josiah's father says, "There are extremes in men" (meaning "in people," of course). Write about two extremes in people that you've noticed. You can write a poem (see the sample under the first fifth/sixth grade topic) or a short essay.

# The Samaritan

Writing Clearly: Using the Senses

**Third/Fourth:**
• Write about a scary encounter you had with an animal. Do this in a six-line poem (which doesn't have to rhyme!), with each of the first five lines using one of the senses and the last one telling how you felt.

> Example:
> Monkey's breath like rotten eggs
> Eyes like glittering marbles
> A high-pitched screech running through my veins
> A leathery little hand on my arm
> The taste of fear on my tongue
> As I went running scared!

• Describe a small child you know, about Dorcas's age, using all five senses.
• If you were tied to a tree near your house and blindfolded like Josiah was, what would your other senses tell you about your surroundings? Start your piece this way: "I'm tied to a tree (or pole) near where I live. There is a blindfold on my eyes so I can't see. . . ."

**Fifth/Sixth Topics:**
• Have you ever experienced an incident in church that made you want to laugh? Describe it using all five of your senses.
• What does it feel like to be lonely? Write a poem that uses all

five senses. Here's an example using *fear*:

> A spider skittering up my arm
> A door slamming in the middle of the night
> The taste of my dry mouth as I wait for the dentist
> The odor of chlorine as I make my first dive from the board
> The darkness when I turn out my light
> AFRAID

- Describe someone you know who is mostly "good" but has one or two "bad" traits, or someone who is mostly "bad" but displays a surprising "good" characteristic here and there. Use all five of your senses in the description.

Seventh/Eighth Topics:
- What do you do when you feel completely alone or abandoned? Describe your actions, using all five of your senses. It can be a five-sentence paragraph.
- Write a poem or five-sentence paragraph with this line as the first: "Until you forgive, you're always alone in your heart." Use all five senses in your piece.
- Keeping Betty Parris, Silas Putnam, and Tituba in mind, write a five-senses poem with this title, "Surprising Friend."

# The Secret

Writing Clearly: Using Action

Third/Fourth Topics:
- Write a list of as many words as you can think of to describe the way a snake moves. If you've never seen a real snake, use another animal with which you're familiar. If I were to use my dog Jake, I would write:

Jake
Romping, dancing, jumping,
racing, chasing, leaping,
bounding, hauling, panting,
loping, prancing, chewing
Jake

- Have you ever been chased by someone or something? Describe the chase. When you're finished, go back and underline every verb (action word) you used. If you used the same one more than once, change it so they're all different.
- It's hard to say good-bye to close friends. Think about a time when you've had to separate from a friend, or imagine what it would be like if you did. Write about it, using seven action words for what's going on *inside* you when you say good-bye. Is your heart pounding? Are you holding back tears? Do you feel all twisted up inside?

**Fifth/Sixth Topics:**
- Observe the way someone moves—your baby sister, your bus driver, your soccer coach, and so on. Describe that movement using only the best 10 action words you can think of—with the last line tying everything together.

Example:
The Old Man Next Door
Shuffles, creeps, stiffens,
stretches, crouches, bends,
hunches, trembles, squints,
sighs.
Just to plant his garden.

- Have you ever been trapped, even for a short time? Describe the experience, using action words explaining what went on *inside* you at the time. Underline all the action words when

you're finished. See if any of them could be changed to make the situation more clear.
- Write a confession for something you've done. Bring it to life with action words.

**Seventh/Eighth Topics:**
- Observe yourself for a day. Then using only action words and the word I, describe the way you move. Add one last line to sum up your movement style.

> Example:
> I stumble
> I trip
> I flail
> I skid
> I crash
> (I burn!)
> I blunder—
> But I get there!

- Josiah's father says, "The answers are seldom black and white. You have to find the right shade of gray in God's will" (p. 57). Write a diary entry about a time you discovered that to be true. Use 10 actions words to describe your turmoil. Underline the action words when you're finished. Use a thesaurus to see if there is a more precise word you could use for each verb.
- Write the word *good-bye* at the top of a piece of paper. Now brainstorm as many action words as come to mind when you think of saying good-bye. List them as fast as you can. Choose the 10 best ones and write any piece (a poem, a descriptive paragraph, a song) you want using those 10 words. Your title is, of course, "Good-bye."

It's been my experience—though yours may differ—that readers' interest in this area runs something like this:

**Third/Fourth graders** are intrigued by the church itself—what it looked like, how the kids were treated, the things they did during the service.

**Fifth/Sixth graders** seem to like the history of the church, especially when it comes to the unfairness and injustice and the way some people fought against that.

**Seventh/Eighth graders** are usually motivated to see how faith applies to them personally.

So in this "folder," I've pointed out for you which parts of each book apply to each level, with some topics you can use for discussion, writing, activities, or projects.

# The Rescue

Third/Fourth:
- Rules for swimming (p. 6)
- Boys in church in Salem Village (pp. 27-34)
- Boys in church in Salem Town (pp. 87-91)
- Differences in churches in town and village (p. 87)

Fifth/Sixth:
- Rules about who can become a member (pp. 30-34)
- Quakers versus Puritans (pp. 44-48)
- Fines for not going to church (pp. 81-83)
- The Puritan belief that all misfortune is God's punishment (pp. 124-125)
- Lecture Day (p. 149)
- Punishment for harboring a heathen (pp. 173-176)

Seventh/Eighth:
- Josiah's father takes a stand against church injustice (p. 59)
- Josiah's father does what he thinks is right even though it's against the church (pp. 110-113)
- Praying when you feel guilty (p. 120)
- A real relationship with God, not just following a bunch of rules (pp. 142-144)
- Josiah finally feels close to God (p. 162)
- Josiah has a few doubts about God (p. 164)
- Taking a stand (pp. 173-180)
- Prayer (p. 185)

# The Stowaway

Third/Fourth:
- Treatment of Puritan girls (p. 12)
- When kids are allowed to touch the Bible (p. 39)
- The mean minister/teacher (p. 53)
- Boys in church in Salem Town (p. 54-64)
- Josiah is allowed to touch the Bible (pp. 166-167)

Fifth/Sixth:
- God's punishment (pp. 12-13)
- Puritan fear of knowledge (p. 131)
- Puritan view of kids (p. 185)

Seventh/Eighth:
- Josiah's father makes up his own mind about wealth (pp. 17-18)
- Josiah goes to God for help (pp. 36-37)
- Feeling too guilty to go to God (pp. 110, 135)
- Going back to God after you've messed up (pp. 135-137)
- Telling someone else about your relationship with God (p. 152)
- Phillip English's spiritual view of wealth (p. 162)
- Josiah goes back to God (p. 194)

# The Guardian

Third/Fourth:
- Obedience to parents (p. 16)
- Josiah, Rebecca, and Reverend Parris in the Meeting House (pp. 106-113)
- When a Puritan dad makes a mistake (p. 121)

**Fifth/Sixth:**
- Puritans versus Indians (pp. 34-35)
- The ideas of the Puritan minister (pp. 109-113)

**Seventh/Eighth:**
- How Josiah's father's choices affect the family (p. 5)
- Everybody has a gift from God (p. 55)
- Figuring things out with God when you've messed up (p. 75)
- What Josiah learned about figuring things out with God (p. 180)

# The Accused

**Third/Fourth:**
- Josiah's dad—different from other Puritan fathers (p. 60)
- What we can learn from the Indians (pp. 128-132, 160-161)

**Fifth/Sixth:**
- The Puritan view of bettering oneself (pp. 9, 24)
- The Puritan's obligation to the minister (p. 10)
- What we can learn from the Indians (pp. 128-132, 160-161)

**Seventh/Eighth:**
- Joseph Hutchinson takes a stand (p. 25)
- When God is easiest to find (p. 82)
- How do you know God is with you? (p. 91)
- How Josiah's dad makes his decisions (p. 101)
- Josiah's discovery about God's presence (p. 146)
- Josiah's prayer (pp. 149-150)
- A promise to God (pp. 195-196)
- A special spot for talking to God (p. 197)
- Josiah applies what he's learned to his life (p. 202)

# The Samaritan

**Third/Fourth:**
- Boys in church (pp. 21-26)
- Children at a funeral (pp. 92-93)

**Fifth/Sixth:**
- Dealing with the poor (pp. 88-89, 108)
- A Puritan minister's view about the church property (p. 98)
- Trouble in Salem Village (p. 207)

**Seventh/Eighth:**
- Background on Josiah's father's stand against the church (pp. 18-19)
- Joseph Hutchinson tries to apply Christian principles to his life (pp. 29-32)
- Josiah also begins trying to apply Christian principles to his life (p. 36)
- Josiah tries to take to heart what he hears in church (p. 93)
- Joseph Putnam's words on forgiveness (p. 96)
- Different interpretations of the Good Samaritan parable (pp. 136-137)
- How Josiah's father lives his life as a Christian (pp. 145-149, 199)
- Josiah follows his father's example (pp. 151, 174)
- How the Christian example can affect someone else's life (p. 205)

# The Secret

Third/Fourth:
- Rules about Puritan kids having boyfriends and girlfriends (p. 62)
- The boys in church at Salem Village (pp. 86-90)

Fifth/Sixth:
- Background on what's been splitting the Salem Village church (p. 16)
- Josiah's father wants to set the church straight (p. 17)
- The minister acts paranoid (p. 36)
- Why the Puritans came to the New World (p. 55)
- How people were treated when they questioned the church (pp. 89-90, 96-98)
- The Puritans' views on sin (p. 162)

Seventh/Eighth:
- Joseph Hutchinson explains how he makes decisions (pp. 55-57)
- Josiah feels close to God (p. 127)
- Hope and Josiah discuss God's will (p. 139)
- The peace of doing His will (p. 152)
- Josiah's father's final decision (pp. 162-163)
- Looking for peace (pp. 171, 183-185)

# Ways-to-Make-It-Matter Folder

These are ideas for pulling it all together once you've completed the entire six-book series. I've offered two suggestions for each grade level, but don't let that number limit you. Allow your imagination to run wild!

### Ideas for Third/Fourth Graders:
- Make a sales poster or booklet for The Salem Years, giving all the reasons why other kids should read the books.
- Pack a bag of mementos Josiah will take with him to Virginia, one from each book. Draw the mementos or sculpt them from clay.

### Ideas for Fifth/Sixth Graders:
- Make a scrapbook for either Hope or Josiah to remind her or him of all they experienced and learned during those six seasons in Salem.
- Write and illustrate a children's picture book depicting all the lessons Josiah learned throughout the series.

Ideas for Seventh/Eighth Graders:
- Put together a Salem Village newspaper. Use your own newspaper for ideas on sections to include.
- Write the complete Puritan Kids' Survival Guide!

Do not hesitate to put the following pages into your copy machine and crank out as many as you like (enlarge them if you can). The top left-hand corner of each sheet will tell you for which subject and grade level the exercise is intended.

History/*The Rescue*
Third/Fourth

## YOU THINK *YOU* HAVE IT ROUGH!

You think your parents make you do a lot of chores?  Go back and check out what Hope and Josiah had to do!  Fill in their chore lists:

Hope's Chores

Josiah's Chores

History/*The Rescue*
Fifth/Sixth


**WHAT DID JOSIAH LEARN...**


About the Indians?  Name three things:

_____

_____

_____


About the Quakers?  Name three things:

_____

_____

_____


About the differences between Salem Town and Salem Village?
Name three:

_____

_____

_____

History/*The Rescue*
Seventh/Eighth

## A DAY IN THE LIFE...

Schedule a typical day in the life of a Puritan kid Josiah and Hope's age in 1690. Don't forget to include what he or she eats.

Kid's name: _____

Before sunrise: _____

_____

_____

At sunrise: _____

_____

_____

After breakfast: _____

_____

_____

At noon: _____

_____

_____

After dinner: _____

_____

_____

_____

At sundown: _____

_____

_____

_____

After supper: _____

_____

_____

_____

History/*The Stowaway*
Third/Fourth

## IT MUST HAVE BEEN FUN BACK THEN!

They had some really cool things in Josiah and Hope's time that we don't have now. Flip through *The Stowaway* and see if you can find five items from the 17th century. Draw a picture of each one.

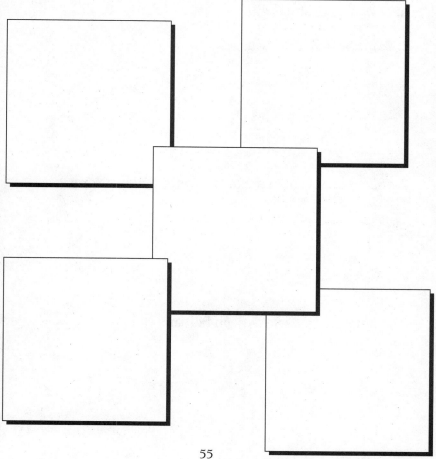

History/*The Stowaway*
Fifth/Sixth


## SCHOOL DAZE

Think about what school was like in Josiah's day. Throughout The Salem Years, he comes into contact with three kinds of schools. Sort them out in the spaces below, identifying and describing in detail why they're different. Which one would you have wanted to attend?

1. Dame School in the village:




2. Grammar School in the town—with Nicholas Noyes:




3. Private tutoring with Joseph Putnam:

History/*The Stowaway*
Seventh/Eighth

## WHAT'S COOKING?

Make a menu from the year 1690, based on what you've learned in *The Stowaway*. For dinner, the main meal of the day, write up two menu options—one to be served in Salem Village and one to be served in Salem Town.

History/*The Guardian*
Third/Fourth

## WHO'S AFRAID OF . . .

Like Josiah—and Rebecca and William and Sarah—just about every kid is afraid of *something*. So go ahead, spill it! Write down one of your fears in each of the spaces below. Draw a picture of each one, too. (Example: If you're afraid of water, you can draw the ocean; if you're afraid of dogs, you can draw a vicious-looking pit bull.) Then fill in the characters' fears—and answer the questions at the bottom of the page.

My three fears:
Fear #1                     Fear #2                     Fear #3

The Salem characters' fears:
Rebecca's Fear          Sarah's Fear              Josiah's Fear

Questions:
1. Are the fears of 17th-century kids any different from yours?

2. Who should we turn to when we're afraid?

History/*The Guardian*
Fifth/Sixth

## ONE-ANSWER WORKSHEET

Every one of these questions has the same answer.  See if you can figure out what it is.

1. Why was Thomas Putnam drilling the soldiers when there were no hostile Indians near Salem Village?

_____

_____

2. Why did the Putnams set traps to kill the wolves?

_____

_____

3. Why did Rebecca run away when she saw the wolf's tail on the door?

_____

_____

4. What is the answer to all the above questions?

_____

_____

History/*The Guardian*
Seventh/Eighth

## DOWN WITH CRUELTY!

We hear a lot these days about violence, cruelty, and injustice—but in many ways, we've got nothing on the 17th-century Puritans! Below you'll find some blank protest signs. Fill in each one with a protest of a cruelty or injustice or instance of ignorance you find in *The Guardian*. Be creative!

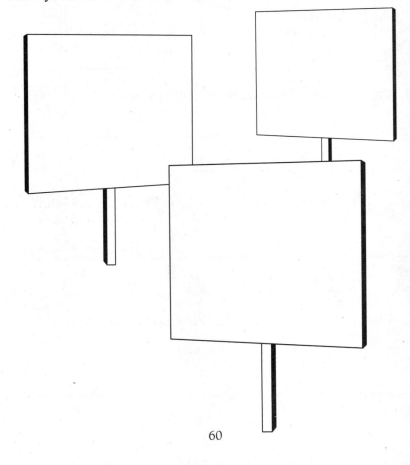

History/*The Accused*
Third/Fourth

## WOULD YOU WANT TO BE A PURITAN KID?

You can't really answer that question until you gather all the information. Fill in the spaces below, then compare and decide.

| Josiah's Chores/Your Chores |
| --- |
| |

| Josiah's Toys/Your Toys |
| --- |
| |

| Josiah's Food/Your Food |
| --- |
| |

| Josiah's Clothes/Your Clothes |
| --- |
| |

| How Josiah Kept Warm/How You Keep Warm |
| --- |
| |

So...do you want to go back and live in the 17th century? Why or why not?

History/*The Accused*
Fifth/Sixth

## POW-WOW!

You've seen stuff in the movies and on TV about Native Americans—but is what you see true? Let's find out. In the spaces below, list the facts you've learned so far about New England Indians from The Salem Years.

• Facts about Indians that you learned from the first Christian Heritage Series:

• Ways the modern media characterize early Native Americans:

• Differences from what you previously thought about Indians:

• Ideas you had that are still true:

Now that you've weighed the similarities and differences, do you think that the movies and TV realistically show what early Native Americans were like? Why or why not?

History/*The Accused*
Seventh/Eighth

## LAW & ORDER

Draw a diagram of the courtroom as described in *The Accused* (pp. 170) and label its parts:

Now draw a diagram of a modern-day courtroom and label *its* parts:

Check out the differences—and similarities!

History/*The Samaritan*
Third/Fourth

## HOMELESS!

There were people without jobs, homes, and food in Josiah's time, just as in ours. The Puritans called them "beggars"; we call them "the homeless." Do we treat them any differently now than they did back then? Let's find out.

1. Find the ways people in *The Samaritan* treated Deliverance Carrier and her little girl and list them under the categories below:

Helpful                          Not Helpful

2. Do the same for the way *we* treat our homeless people now. You might need a grown-up to help you:

Helpful                          Not Helpful

3. So have we improved in the way we treat the poor? Explain your answer.

History/*The Samaritan*
Fifth/Sixth

## PURITAN PICTURE ENCYCLOPEDIA

Write an explanation for each one of these Puritan terms and draw an illustration to go with it.

1. Beating the bounds:

Bonus: What's another word for it? _____

2. Sleeping tight:

Bonus: What's the rest—"sleep tight and _____."

3. Bear pit:

Bonus: What did the Merry Band catch in theirs?

History/*The Samaritan*
Seventh/Eighth

## DOWNHILL!

Josiah's father said the Christian society his father had envisioned was going downhill. Help Mr. Hutchinson explain this to Josiah by listing five ways society had changed for the worse:

1.

2.

3.

4.

5.

History/*The Secret*
Third/Fourth

## JOSIAH, THE SURVIVOR!

In almost every one of the six books, Josiah pulls something from his pouch to help him get out of trouble. In the spaces provided next the pouch picture below, fill in his "lifesavers." The first one is done for you.

*a whistle*
_____
Book 1


_____
Book 2


_____
Book 3


_____
Book 4


_____
Book 5


_____
Book 6

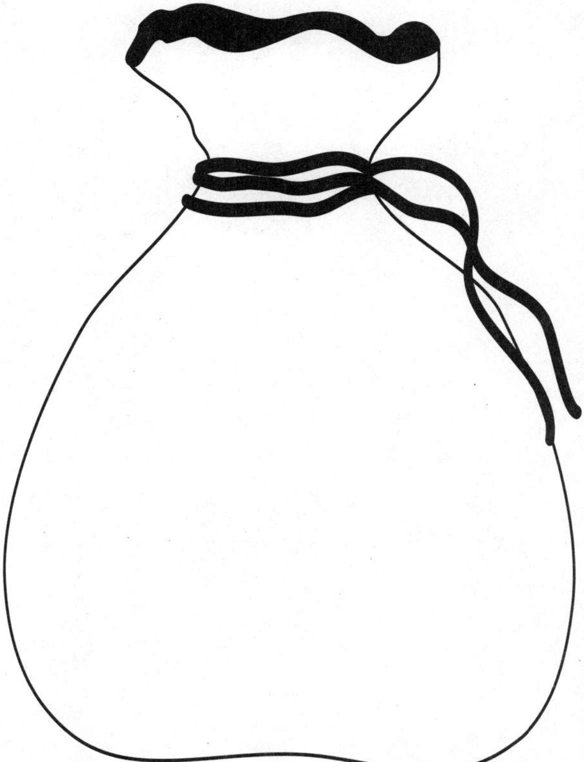

History/*The Secret*
Fifth/Sixth


**POOR REVEREND PARRIS!**

The real Reverend Parris was very much like the one in our books. He spent most of his time worrying about whether people respected him—and as a result, they didn't! Make a list of all the things the minister accused the people of in *The Secret*:

History/*The Secret*
Seventh/Eighth

## NO TRESPASSING!

Those 17th-century landowners were definitely paranoid about people trying to steal or damage their property! Write down all the ways they tried to protect or mark their land, either in *The Secret* or in any of the other books in The Salem Years.

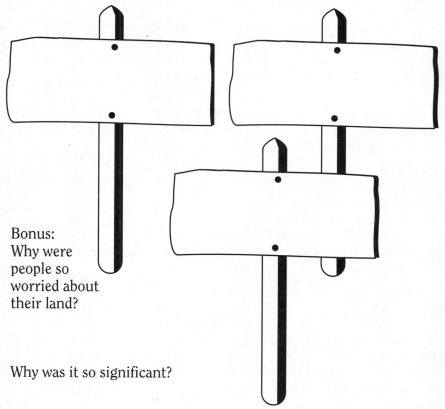

Bonus:
Why were
people so
worried about
their land?

Why was it so significant?

Literature/Plot
*The Rescue*
Third/Fourth

OOPS!

Listed below are some important events that occur in *The Rescue*. A few key elements are missing, though. See if you can fill those in—because without them, there would be no story!

Josiah is following his sister, Hope, and her friends and almost drowns in the Ipswich River. An Indian boy named Oneko saves him and takes Josiah to the Widow Hooker's cabin. At church the next day, Josiah's parents are not _____.

Josiah becomes friends with Oneko and the Widow and learns that, like the Hutchinsons, the Widow has also been mistreated. The next Sunday, Josiah's family goes to _____.
On the way home, the wagon gets stuck in the mud, Hope goes flying out, and Josiah isn't able to help his father. He feels more and more like a brainless boy.

When Josiah's father sends him to the river with Ezekiel to gather stones for the sawmill, instead he and Ezekiel _____. They are discovered there by _____.
She makes Josiah promise to_____.

Soon after, Josiah follows Hope to _____.
She becomes ill and _____ carries her back as far as the field. Hope gets sicker and sicker, and nothing helps—not even the doctor can cure her. So Josiah goes_____.
Oneko carries the Widow to Josiah's house and is nearly caught by one of the Putnams.

Josiah's father allows Widow Hooker to_____.
When Josiah's father takes him to the Widow's cabin for more
supplies, Josiah sees _____. On the way home,
Edward Putnam tells them that Oneko _____.

Meanwhile, the fever has caused Hope to lose her _____,
but thanks to the Widow, she's much better. Yet when it's time to
take Widow Hooker home, she _____.

After the funeral, Hope and Josiah stay to gather the Widow's
belongings and are "kidnapped" by _____.
On their way home, Hope and Josiah discover their father being
put in the stocks. Israel Porter comes along and _____.

Josiah's father tells him that in the summer, he will go
_____. Now Josiah no longer feels like a
_____ _____.

Literature/Plot
*The Rescue*
Fifth/Sixth

## THE PLOT THICKENS!

Fill in this plot line as you and your teacher or class fill in the one in your classroom.

Literature/Plot
*The Rescue*
Seventh/Eighth

## MAJOR CONFLICT!

Person versus nature

Josiah versus the _____(Ch. 1)

Josiah versus the _____(Ch. 9)

Hope versus the _____(Ch. 12)

Person versus person

Josiah versus _____(Ch. 1, 7, 10)

Josiah versus _____(Ch. 8)

Josiah's father versus _____( Ch. 5, 8)

Josiah versus _____(Ch. 7, 10)

Person versus society

Josiah & the boys versus _____(Ch. 4)

Josiah's parents versus _____(Ch. 4, 9, 11, 14, 15)

Widow Hooker versus _____(Ch. 6)

Indians versus _____(Ch. 15)

Person versus himself

Josiah versus feeling like_____

Bonus: Which of these conflicts is resolved in *The Rescue*?

Literature/Setting
*The Stowaway*
Third/Fourth

## WHERE ARE WE?

These are the main locations in Salem Town. See if you can label these places on the map.

1. Phillip English's mansion
2. Christ Church
3. Phillip English's warehouse
4. Point of Rocks
5. English's shop

6. Salem Harbor
7. Shallop Cove
8. *The Hutchinson*
9. *The Adventure*

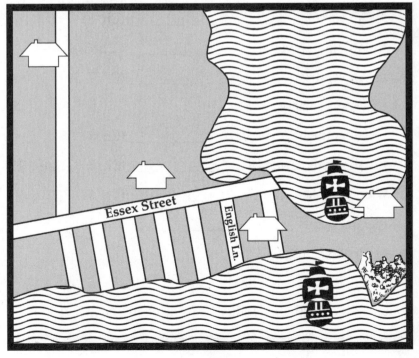

Literature/Setting
*The Stowaway*
Fifth/Sixth

## IN MY MIND...

Sometimes the author will describe a place briefly and leave the rest for you to create in your mind. Allow your imagination to fill in the details of each setting. Then choose one and draw a picture of it.

• The Hutchinsons' best room (p. 19)

• The Hutchinsons' kitchen (p. 30)

• Christ Church in Salem Town (pp. 55-56)

• The Englishes' kitchen (pp. 73-74)

• Phillip English's warehouse (p. 77)

• The Englishes' best room, used for Josiah's schoolroom (p. 91)

• The Englishes' shop (p. 98)

• Simon's cabin on the forecastle deck (pp. 122-123)

• The captain's cabin on the newly-built galleon (p. 147)

Literature/Setting
*The Stowaway*
Seventh/Eighth

## NEW EYES

After he returns from his studies in Salem Town, Josiah sees his home with new eyes. List below some of the details he notices on page 166. The first one's done for you.

1. sound of the leaves brushing together

2. _____

3. _____

4. _____

5. _____

Now imagine you've been away from a place where you feel at home. You're back now. List the details you see with new eyes as you look around.

1. _____

2. _____

3. _____

4. _____

5. _____

Literature/Character
*The Guardian*
Fifth/Sixth

## CHARACTER MAP

Set up a sheet like this on a long piece of paper. As you finish each chapter, write down new information you've discovered about each character. The characters from the first chapter are already listed for you. Continue adding characters and details about them as you read.

• Josiah

• Hope

• Joseph Putnam

• William

• Ezekiel

• Nathaniel

• Jonathon

Literature/Character
*The Guardian*
Seventh/Eighth

## DYNAMIC?  OR  STATIC?

Characters Who Change                    Characters Who Don't

As described in the activity section, now choose two characters you think have changed between the beginning of *The Rescue* and the end of *The Guardian*—and two characters who have remained stubbornly the same. Trace the changes (or describe the lack of changes) using pictures, drawings, phrases from the book, and your own words.

Literature/Point of View
*The Accused*
Third/Fourth

## HOW DID JOSIAH FEEL WHEN...

• His father sent him out to deliver wood? (Chapter 1) _____

_____

• John Indian carried him into the Reverend Parris's home?
(Chapter 3) _____

• Joseph Putnam wouldn't tell him what was wrong? (Chapter 5)

_____

• His father caught him bringing wood from the barn? (Chapter 8)

_____

• Everyone decided that Josiah, rather than Ezekiel, should be
the leader? (Chapter 10) _____

• He thought Ezekiel was in the burning building? (Chapter 12)

_____

• Hope didn't confess her part? (Chapter 15) _____

• Abigail described the jail to him? (Chapter 16) _____

• William, Sarah, and Hope appeared in court? (Chapter 19) ___

_____

• He saw Oneko for the last time? (Chapter 20) _____

_____

Literature/Point of View
*The Accused*
Fifth/Sixth

## WHAT IF SOMEONE ELSE TOLD THE STORY?

Pick one or more of these exercises:

1. Hope writes in her diary when Josiah goes off to court without her.

2. Jonathon Putnam draws a picture of Josiah and the courtroom scene to show to one of his friends who couldn't come to the trial. (He plans to use it later as a dartboard.)

3. Ezekiel writes a letter to Joseph Putnam, explaining himself so the teacher won't think he's a miserable coward.

4. Wolf's wife draws pictures on her cave wall for Oneko, illustrating Josiah's predicament.

Literature/Point of View
*The Accused*
Seventh/Eighth

## FROM A CERTAIN POINT OF VIEW...

PART ONE: Describe the night the fence came down (chapters 12 and 13) from somebody else's point of view—either orally, speaking as the character; in writing; in a comic strip; or using any other creative method you can devise. Remember, the key is to explain things from a different person's perspective. Some point of view options might be: William's, Ezekiel's, Jonathon Putnam's, Eleazer Putnam's, Abigail's (as she heard it from Jonathon), or Hope's (as she heard it from Josiah).

PART TWO: Think of an incident that's happened at school, home, or church. Compare your rendition of what happened—orally or in written or picture form—with that of someone else who was there. You'll see that point of view matters in life as well as in literature!

Literature/Style
*The Samaritan*
Third/Fourth

## STYLE CHECKLIST

The author describes places (check one):
_____using a lot of words
_____using a few words
_____she doesn't describe places

The author writes in (check one):
_____all short sentences
_____all long sentences
_____sentences of different lengths

There is dialogue (check one):
_____on every page
_____on most pages
_____on very few pages

The author makes you (check all the ones that are true):
_____see things
_____hear things
_____smell things
_____taste things
_____think about things
_____feel things, like sadness or anger or
disappointment or excitement

Write a description of something fun—your teacher's nose, your best friend's laugh, or your own big toes. Then do the checklist on your own writing style.

Literature/Style
*The Samaritan*
Fifth/Sixth

## DO YOU HAVE STYLE?

1. How does the author describe Josiah holding little Dorcas's hand when she slips in the mud? (pp. 45-46)

_____

_____


2. Now describe holding a football player's hand when he slips, using the same style. Just fill in the blanks:

He [Josiah] took off toward the cabin with_____in tow, but they didn't go two steps before his_____feet flew out from under him and he was_____at the end of his hand like a_____.


3. The author likes to use vivid, specific verbs. Find eight good ones on pages 116-117:

_____     _____

_____     _____

_____     _____

_____     _____

4. She likes adverbs, too—especially the ones that end in "ly." Find six good ones on pages 86-87:

_____  _____  _____

_____  _____  _____

5. She also likes to write physical descriptions that show what people are feeling. For example:

"Sarah's pale eyes grew wide." (She was scared.)
"William licked his chops." (He was anticipating.)
"The bed curtains whipped back, and Hope glared down at her brother." (She was annoyed.)

Now, using verbs and adverbs, write a physical description for each of these feelings:

(She was disappointed.) _____

(He was surprised.) _____

(They were enraged.) _____

Literature/Style
*The Samaritan*
Seventh/Eighth

## THE STYLE POLICE

Do a little detective work:

1. Read page 72. List the five best verbs on that page.

_____    _____    _____

_____    _____

Write one sentence to describe the way the author uses verbs:

_____

_____

2. Read page 156. List four "ly" adverbs on that page:

_____   _____   _____   _____

Complete this sentence: The author uses "ly" adverbs to

_____.

3. Read pages 181-182. What is Josiah feeling? Try to describe it in no more than three words:

_____   _____   _____

How do you know that's what he's feeling? How does Nancy Rue's style show you that?_____

_____

4. A simile is a comparison of two things using the words *like* or *as*. For example, page four describes, "Like the top crust of a pie, the grass caved in." And on page five, Josiah describes Jonathon as "tall, lanky, and lurking like a thief." The author loves to use similies—they're part of her style. Find 10 more in *The Samaritan* and list them below with their page numbers.

_____

_____

_____

_____

_____

5. On page 84, Nancy Rue writes, "Almost a week passed and there was still no sign of Deliverance Carrier. The Hutchinsons' little guest began to fall into a routine—most of it made up of following Josiah around the farm." Using your own style—one that's comfortable for you—describe little Dorcas getting in Josiah's way. Look back at your style—and describe it!

_____

_____

_____

_____

_____

Literature/Theme
*The Secret*
Third/Fourth

## SECRETS!

1. What secrets did Josiah learn about:

Hope: _____

Giles: _____

Silas: _____

Abigail: _____

Ann: _____

Jonathon, Eleazer, and Richard: _____

2. Have you ever overheard a secret you weren't supposed to hear? Tell about it or draw a picture illustrating the situation.

3. Have you ever spotted someone doing something wrong—and they didn't see you watching them? Write about it or draw a picture.

4. Have you ever kept a secret for someone? Describe or illustrate it.

5. Have you ever talked someone into telling you a secret? Tell about it or draw a picture.

6. Did you ever keep a secret—and wish you hadn't? Write about or draw the experience.

Literature/Theme
*The Secret*
Fifth/Sixth

## HOW DO I KNOW WHAT THE AUTHOR IS TRYING TO SAY?

1. Josiah has one goal in chapters 1, 2, and 3. What is it?
   To find out _____.

2. Then in chapters 4 and 5, his attention switches to another person. He now begins to wonder_____.

3. These questions make it hard for Josiah to make decisions. Should he help Hope? Should he tell his father what he suspects about Giles? In chapter 6, his father gives him some advice. He says before Josiah makes a decision, he must _____

   _____.

4. So Josiah makes a decision and acts on it in chapter 7. But in chapter 8, he starts to feel _____.
   Yet on page 77, something changes his mind. He sees_____

   _____.

5. Events in chapters 9 and 10 change Josiah's mind about helping Hope again. He decides to _____because

   _____.

6. When he sees Reverend Parris's parchment on Giles's desk in chapter 11, Josiah decides to _____ because_____.

7. In chapter 14, Hope and Josiah talk about the things they don't like about themselves. What are they? _____

_____

_____

8. In chapter 16, Josiah and Hope's father explains to them why he thinks they should leave Salem Village. What's his reason?

_____

_____

9. In the last few pages, Josiah's father explains things in a way Josiah can understand. What does he say? _____

_____

_____

10. Look back over all your answers and see what story they tell. What's the one-sentence lesson they all point to?_____

_____

_____

# A Word
# from the Author

I love to hear from readers, and I almost always answer their letters. Feel free to encourage your students to get in touch with me:

Nancy Rue
P.O. Box 3313
Lebanon, TN 37088
E-mail: NANCYRUE@aol.com

FOCUS ON THE FAMILY®

# Other Outstanding Resources *for Teachers*

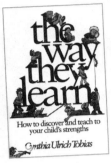

How to discover and teach to
your child's strengths

*Cynthia Ulrich Tobias*

### The Way They Learn

Unlock the potential in your students! By identifying a
wide variety of learning styles, Cynthia Ulrich Tobias
reveals how you can use a child's natural strengths,
interests, and abilities to enhance their education.
A great way to improve performance!

### Teachers in Focus magazine

As you shape the minds and hearts
of tomorrow's leaders, you need
the insight and updates this
magazine provides. Its 32 full-
color pages are packed with inspiring arti-
cles and innovative ideas you're sure to find
helpful. Plus, it's issued nine times a year (correspon-
ding to the traditional school year), so you'll receive
the encouragement you want when you need it.

•  •  •

## *. . . and Students!*

Great literature is timeless—it upholds traditional values and transcends the
years like few things do. And unlike any other series on the market,
**Focus on the Family's "Classic Collection"** is truly unique! Selected for the
quality of its content and the value in its message, every classic tale features:

- the Christian content other editions often omit
- the complete text, updated for easier reading
- student-tested discussion questions that help readers get the most out
  of each inspiring novel
- woodcut illustrations from the book's original printing
- an in-depth introduction detailing the people, places and historical
  events that influenced the author and surround the story

The series features *Little Women, Ben-Hur,
A Christmas Carol* and *Robinson Crusoe.*

•  •  •

For more information or to request any of these resources, simply write to
Focus on the Family, Colorado Springs, CO 80995, or call 1-800-A-FAMILY
(1-800-232-6459). Friends in Canada may write to Focus on the Family, P.O.
Box 9800, Stn. Terminal, Vancouver, B.C. V6B 4G3, or call 1-800-661-9800.
Visit our Web site—www.family.org—to learn more about the ministry or
to find out if there is a Focus on the Family office in your country.